KICKING SAWDUST

Also by Paul Hyland

POETRY

Riddles for Jack (Northern House, 1978)
Domingus (Mid-Day Publications, 1978)
Poems of Z (Bloodaxe Books, 1982)
The Stubborn Forest (Bloodaxe Books, 1984)

TRAVEL & TOPOGRAPHY

Purbeck: The Ingrained Island (Gollancz, 1978;
   Dovecote, 1989)
Wight: Biography of an Island (Gollancz, 1984)
The Black Heart: A Voyage into Central Africa
   (Gollancz, 1988; Holt, 1989; Paragon House, 1990)
Indian Balm: Travels in the Southern Subcontinent
   (HarperCollins, 1994; Flamingo, 1995)

OTHER

Getting into Poetry (Bloodaxe Books, 1992)

Paul Hyland

KICKING
SAWDUST

*for Margaret & Ben
with thanks for your welcome
and best wishes for your walk...*

Paul Hyland

10 × 97

BLOODAXE BOOKS

ISBN: 1 85224 312 0

First published 1995 by
Bloodaxe Books Ltd,
P.O. Box 1SN,
Newcastle upon Tyne NE99 1SN.

Bloodaxe Books Ltd acknowledges
the financial assistance of Northern Arts.

Cover printing by J. Thomson Colour Printers Ltd, Glasgow.

Printed in Great Britain by
Cromwell Press Ltd, Broughton Gifford, Melksham, Wiltshire.

To Ydidiah and the Magi
at Mogultur

Acknowledgements

Most of the poems in this book are published here for the first time but I wish to thank the editors and producers of the following publications and programmes in which some of them first appeared: Company of Poets' *Taboo* (Blue Button Press, 1993), *Cornish Links* (Kernow Poets Press, 1993 & 1995), *Once-and-Future Portugal* (BBC Radio 3), *The Poetry Book Society Anthology 1987-1988* (PBS/Hutchinson, 1987), *Poetry Now* (BBC Radio 3), *Poetry Wales*, *Smoke*, *Tremor in the Raven's Throat* (BBC Radio 4), and *Wight: Biography of an Island* (Victor Gollancz, 1984).

'Wormwood' I wrote on hearing an item about the aftermath of the Chernobyl disaster on BBC Radio 4's *From Our Own Correspondent*. The *Daily Telegraph* (so I later learned from a note in Ken Smith's *Wormwood*) made some mischief with the story and was denounced by the bishop of Kiev. However, the BBC report I had heard was subsequently confirmed and I checked the meaning of *chernobyl* in Ukrainian (thanks to Karen Hayes and Andrew Lachowitz). *Pace* Ken Smith, it seems that the CIA's sense of humour was redundant in this case.

Finally, I am grateful to Sir Philip Astley, who, with an amphitheatre that began as a ring of hoof prints in 1768, helped me to kick some sawdust in a book now published under his descendant's imprint.

Contents

The more you practise the better you'll sing,
the more you groan the sicker you'll become.

TELUGU PROVERB

We must surrender our hopes and expectations, as well
as our fears, and march directly into disappointment...

CHÖGYAM TRUNGPA

Happy the specialist! He hasn't enough time
for his limited domain. If I were to live again,
I would be happy to study nothing but termites.

ANDRÉ GIDE

Ovid Plastering

To be candid
it's better than sentry duty
in the unspeakable Black Sea winter

Do not believe
all you read in my *Tristia*
though my hand is cold on this wet trowel

The masonry
provincial but sound enough
a bed for my apprentice upward strokes

The art of love
must be renounced reluctantly
only when *Remedia Amoris* fail

In far Rome once
I saw Virgil but didn't speak
regrets unaccountable and precious

It's not prison
this room I am making a world
choosing to live where fate has exiled me

I like the thought
of wet gypsum's blank expanses
after some practice I'll love the finish

With a damp brush
and steel I burnish it bone-white
then paint on it endlessly with my mind

I watch it dry
patchily like the beach or clouds
changing and changing into perfection

Love & Death, All the Minutiae
(Athens)

Generations flit past
like beads on a rosary:
the snick of the latch
the tunc of the hammer

the abacus tots up the cost.
The penis enters, bidden
bidden and bidden again.
Between are shadows. In them

women are deeper shadows
nursing invisible flames.
The men burn, hands flickering,
worry-beads clacking like crickets.

Bicycles

(at Oradour-sur-Glane 1994)

There is no more useless thing
than a twisted bicycle,
unless it's two of them hung
from one nail in the wall:

three warped wheels
a necklace of rusty chain
a crossbar and four pedals
like rudimentary limbs,

crankshaft locked solid
with fifty years' weather
beyond the blaze that shrugged
off tiles and lifted rafters.

Exposed, these bicycles
are frail and wiry, faintly
human mechanicals
half gone, linked gently

– pedals to feet
handlebars to hands
saddle to seat –
by nothing more than

memories, useless ones
of that summer afternoon
when the inhabitants
were herded to the green,

men into barns, women
and children into church;
this place an empty lane
an overcrowded ditch.

13

Near Guernica

My teeth meet through a thick tortilla
inside the café of deep silence
on the road to Miranda de Ebro.

The coffee is darkest arabica
tilted at narrow whispering faces,
the blood most likely of group O

and Rhesus negative. Men's boiler
suits are plangent blue, shirts sonorous
grey, somewhere a secretive radio

and in relief on the wall, Guernica,
carved and burnished woodwork that owes
everything but beauty to Picasso.

The lightbulb has a warm patina,
the hybrid bull glows, the screaming horse
is a well-polished palomino.

I am eating food off an altar,
gazing at an unholy reredos
with peaked flames instead of a halo.

Here, where strangeness is familiar
the sword snaps, the turned lamp gutters
and today's long-buried voices grow

suddenly raucous. Workmen's laughter
lifts words, music from the Caucasus
perhaps, from the east and long ago.

Wormwood

This is a martial herb, and is governed by Mars.
CULPEPER

*And the third angel sounded, and there fell a great star from heaven,
burning as it were a lamp... And the name of the star is called
wormwood: and the third part of the waters became wormwood;
and many men died of the waters, because they were made bitter.*
REVELATION 8, 10 & 11

This plant belongs to Mars.
It grows on the banks of the Dnieper.
In low potency it cures
nervous tremors, deliriums,
hallucinations, terrors
and poisoning by mushrooms.
Its leaves are grey and downy
and it is bitter.

It blooms in June and July
on waste land in dry regions
and thrives on the banks of the Dnieper.
As *absinthe* it engenders
nervous tremors, deliriums,
hallucinations, terrors,
in excess. In moderation
it is a tonic.

It sends Soviet citizens
back to their bibles,
communists and christians
suffering tremors and terrors,
the bitter text: in Ukrainian
'wormwood' is *chernobyl*.
Chernobyl on the banks of the Dnieper.
This plant belongs to Mars.

Picture of Nobody
(El Salvador)

A picture full of women and
one man in a picture in the picture.
One woman holds the frame but
we cannot see her hands
we cannot see the lap
that bears the man, the icon.

Next to her a comrade hides
her eyes with a bent hand.
Behind her the women grow
indistinct, massed, as if miles
of women pressed up to the lens
this focus, this man whose eyes

fix us. The others cast down.
Here is sorrow, anguish, outrage
he is not part of. He is absent
is disappeared, he is the man
child slipping from the grasp
of the angry, mourning virgin.

Articulating Hungary
(1956-1989)

Imre Nagy is excavated
watched by his daughter and granddaughter
bone by bone from the unmarked grave
where he was thrown face-down.

Bone by bone: pelvis, scapula, jaw,
skull like mahogany, tibia and fibula
like twigs still rooted in boots,
laced boots that trod the air.

    Elsewhere a woman disinters
    a shirt from her drawer;
    says she's washed it, washed it
    but stains stay where the bullet
    tore from her husband's chest,
    a family secret until now.

Two hundred thousand witness
Nagy's funeral, his skeleton assembled
face-up in a pristine casket,
a revolution resurrected.

    The woman holds out the shirt:
    a banner, a flag kept folded
    for the day she would be free
    to fly it, heavy words
    tearing out of her mouth faster
    and faster, lighter and lighter.

Imre Nagy: installed in government by USSR, premier 1953-55 and in 1956
uprising, seized by Russian troops and hung in 1958, reburied 1989.

Dom Sebastião, King of Portugal

(after Fernando Pessoa)

Mad, yes, mad, for I wanted majesty
such as Fate never allows.
My conviction did not fit within me;
that's why where the desert lies
my has-been self remained, not he who is.

My madness, let others take it from me
and all that went with it.
Without madness what can man be
other than a healthy brute,
a postponed corpse that procreates?

Dom Sebastião died in battle with the emperor of Morocco at
Ksar-el-Kebir in 1578. Tradition has it that he, 'the one-that-is',
will return as saviour of the Portuguese.

Dom Sebastião's Song

(Cape St Vincent)

He who goes to search for the bride in the noise of war
dies without bride and without love, quite alone.'
MIGUEL TORGA

Maybe, O shaman, your glance shall discern
the ship in which the hidden one must return.
ANTÓNIO SARDINHA

And how shall I come back from the dark
I who walked off the end of the world
crossed the sea's abyss to disembark
into the desert's impossible odds?

How then shall I come back from the dead
weapons burnished by the building sands
my supposed bones, rifled by wind, hid
in the gilded dune's reliquary?

How shall I take up my plundered pack
how shall I wake from a soldier's sleep
guitarra whose slack strings vultures pluck
to wake my lover who thinks me dead?

How arouse her who dreams me standing
beyond black water, both arms blessing
with, from my loins, a pontoon springing
sturdy bridge to carry her across?

How wake my lover who dreams me dead
gem in her casket, skull like amber
bleached and stretched on her ironing board
on her arm, walking, flesh round my feet?

How, like St Vincent, sail relics home
how harness ravens to this wreckage
how, in my lover's own time, return
wake the bereaved and waste their grieving?

My dreams of blood, the desert's ashes
sackcloth of sand and shame in battle
I'll renounce for a sailor's habit
and the dumb dunes for the prayerful swell.

My destination thyme and bugloss
stonechats' chime on the promontory
the rose of winds shall be my compass
westwards, a sunk sun boiling the sea.

Covered in darkness, swathed in sea-mist
unpierced by the navigator's gaze
by poet's eye or sacred lighthouse
I'll moor my wraith beneath the fortress.

Sleep on, my rival, landfall soft now
where the sea ends and the earth begins
I'll tiptoe home to my own pillow
surprise myself in my lover's arms.

Loquat Song

O the loquats Rosalinha
    plucks me from her backyard tree,
Teeth must try, and find their skins are
    taut and tart and tempting me.

How the flesh bursts on my palate,
    how the juice burns on my tongue.
Laughs Rosalinha – You must wait! –
    so I wait, too long, too long.

Her thick legs and crop-soiled fingers
    are decked out in black, in black;
On her lips a girl's smile lingers,
    lover's lustre in her look.

While beneath the stern green foliage
    fruit grows golden with the sun,
My plucked loquats die of old age,
    brown and wrinkled, on the wane.

But I mouthe a sour-plum, split her
    and am ravished with delight.
When they're ripened, O how bitter,
    when they're rotten, O how sweet

Like men's souls and like men's sins are,
    like the fruits of purgatory;
O the loquats Rosalinha
    plucks me from her backyard tree.

The Tradition of Discovery
(Costa Nova, Portugal)

How the breakers muster force
from the Atlantic's breadth.
This gravitas between continents
weighs upon a lost land-mass
booms and sighs in the long sands
like dreams that lift, shrug, overtake sleep.

The sun voyages westwards, its aura
highlights everything's edges: this shore
a strand between river and sea,
footing for the precarious town,
its young poised on the margin.
Two are posed, now, in the surf's lace.

The white floes of her dress and veil
wash around, between, the darker legs
of his dark suit. They embrace,
leap and laugh at the big waves.
Their wedding flowers burn in the sun
and, doused, glisten with brine.

These moments the photographer takes;
his tripod's legs lapped in foam bear
the scene's weight, the still edge, the timeless
flowers. Two, close and shining. Between,
a sun, an ocean. The shutter's snick
discovers a continent rising.

The Pangs of Words

Years on I feel again, again the shock
of your slow dying and your death –
if the possessive adjective applies.
Yours became ours. All your friends mourned.
I grieved for you but not, I think, enough.

Heart-sickness that ambushes me today
is not old ravening grief
but love which your death and my life betrayed;
love which we had and would not hold
because you had a man and I a wife.

It was denial but not punishment.
Which hurts most, past tense or passive
mood? For far too long I've framed the words
my mouth last printed on your skin.
Now I mourn me you loved, and you in health.

I'll celebrate you whole to cure myself:
your pressure, colour, smell. My love
– if the possessive adjective applies –
you knew the pangs of words; that grief
does not quite rhyme with death, nor love with life.

Invisible Ink

Here are the love letters I've not written.
Bring your face close and breathe
the slight perfume imbuing each unsent page,
something of soil, rain, something of flowers.
Watch the snow sheet. Writing unravels
like wire that runs away into the wood
and over the hill. See telegraph poles
sprout roots and branches, the trees whispering.

See lightnings flare along the horizon
and ink in all the nerve-ends of the skin.
Close your eyes, listen, the wires run deep
down beyond the skyline, poles tall, nerves taut,
branches and roots, roots and branches like nets
snaring the rocks, our clouds. Searching. Leafing.
Open your eyes, see how the floor is filling
with all the love letters I've not written.

Room Enough

Perhaps this room begins
as a cupboard where toys
fall over themselves to
spill into light of play
or huddle on the night's
shadowy floor, yearning
to be tidied away.

Perhaps it is a closet
sparse with sacred creatures
ebony wand, gold ring
snakeskin and hollow bone
alert for their fleshing,
too awful to open
without lips frame their spell.

Or a room with a bed
where long lithe bodies meet
where hungry mouths swap tongues
where words are swallowed down
distilled to their juices
erotic essences
while the minds go hunting.

Perhaps it detaches
itself from the kitchen
the study, the garden.
Perhaps the room floats free
and we fleshy spirits
fumble for the pass-key
to cupboard, closet, vault.

Our hands land on the latch
offer each the penthouse
the stable-suite, the barn
in which tamed wild things rut
for our domestication
where deft spiders weave and
bats wing of their own will.

Now we have found a room
in the wind between rains
between wood and midden
under the holly bush
under the light we lie
naked with our clothes on
or off, our hair falling.

Here we caress our pelts
here words enter our ears
here eyes flame clear, flesh weeps
pursed and pierced, soft as felt
hilt hard against bone-shield
whole skins incandescent
sun shafts, here in this room.

Now it chooses its walls
as the mind the brain-pan
as the body its bones
as whole meets whole and grows
so that it terrifies
whatever's left outside
embraces all we know.

It is complete, but keeps
asking for completeness.
The wind kicks the door in
curtains flail like ghost flags
flushing the room of us
I quail, you moan but it's
your cheek my tears dry on.

In the morning we leave
the room empty, the world
larger for us, but small.
Each re-enters thinking
the other is still there.
Each, alarmed, has to love
the world where we still are.

This not the recipe
for ruin, monument
to love. This not a shell
but dome split open for
the dance of little deaths
that with the elements
storms, storms the open door.

Reprieve

Though wanting me, you granted a reprieve
and ran for sweet life, swearing that you'd stay:
you loved so dearly that you had to leave.

You wore my heart for months upon your sleeve
but in your marrow sensed an old dismay.
Though wanting me you granted a reprieve

I hadn't asked, for how should I conceive
of such desire wishing itself away?
You loved, so dearly that you had to leave

me sick and angry that you could deceive,
committing yourself only to betray,
though wanting, me. You granted a reprieve

from your dark dreams, intricate and naive,
which tangled love with death and night with day;
you loved so dearly that you had to leave.

You hated to destroy or undeceive
yourself and me, but chose to end the play:
though wanting me you granted a reprieve,
you loved so dearly that you had to leave.

Firework

(for Tom)

Yesterday, your second birthday,
recalled how your dad rang my bell
at midnight to announce you.
For you he would have chimed
a steepleful.

Last night I dreamt of him, not fit
as memory has him but as he became:
wasted, still on his feet. I woke
to the fresh shock and the relief
that he is not.

I set off fireworks in his place
tonight. You liked the colours, red,
green, golden flares, but rockets
rushing skywards made you cry.
You're safe, we said.

Then, in the comfortable dark
as our small bonfire ebbed and died,
the last one dropped back silently
and rapped my shoulder hard
scattering sparks.

Long Shot

A stone house opens its black door
expels a boy into its ground.
He vaults a rhine, runs at the wind

takes hawthorn hedges in his stride
by stile or gate or gap and shakes
flecks of their spume into his wake.

Clouds' shadows shoal inland beneath
green corn that bows and never breaks,
dark reefs ridden by hawthorns' surf;

they seem to speed the boy whose feet
make of ploughs' jetsam stepping-stones
across the choppy furrows' foam.

What stops him is the pebble ridge,
shifty thunderous bastion
whose stones he loves in the low sun:

moon-gems, great eggs and polished grain
he harvests till his arms are full.
Smooth scree gives way to sand and swell.

Feet in the salt he crouches now,
unlooses stone by stone. Each one
careens toward the bald horizon

each shaves white heads and mows green mounds,
each is interred. Each shout – *Fly! Fly!* –
wind-blown, rides homeward and is drowned.

Spent, the boy turns. Sandprints' long strides
carry him back, ridge, furrow, stone,
wave upon wave of broken thorn.

No Before or After

To this, there's no before or after.
It stands between delirium and
delirium, hole in a frosted pane,
a window out of time. And not a dream.

I see, close up, above the picture rail,
fine cracks and paper puckered where walls
meet ceiling at the corner of my room.
No nightmare this. Cracks do not open.

I seem to turn and look down on my bed
whose rumpled covers are like ripples
cast into relief by window-shine,
the curtains slightly swaying, and frozen.

It's no surprise it's my face on the pillow;
my mother bends and blots it out, bathing
my brow, the doctor times my pulse, his hair
is thinning, reads the thermometer

he has just taken from between my lips,
lays my arm down and shakes his head. I
can feel none of this. I see it all.
I can see care, so clearly. Then I fall.

Stone Age

(for Jane Lees, Avebury)

In your dad's fields, megaliths grew like mushrooms
Big stones like planets hovered in deep meadow

Cows rubbed at elementary particles
orbiting your eccentric nucleus

Now you mock strangers who stretch dowsers' hands
to touch with arcane intimacy holy things

You smile at how – innocent of their potency
of neolithic physics and metaphysics –

you scaled them all, straddled them and slid down
knickers in holes, how your mum scolded you

Place-Setting

But did you tell me how slime stank
when you cleared up and packed things clean away?
I know you talked of you all afternoon
in Richmond, in your girlhood's house:
your mother buried but not exorcised,
your father pacing carpets far upstairs,
the plumbing's immured sssh! and hisst!

Something stays. You told me how the Thames
rose up one day to flood the cellar.
How, in that dark, unknown to you
the long-stored wedding-day bone china
was buoyed up. It lifted with the tide,
then fell where you would find it whole
and dazzlingly arrayed upon the mud.

Right of Passage

(Parkstone)

I liked the street I played in
as a kid, but for one house
that lurked behind its trees,
peered over unpruned shrubs
and overgrown weed beds:
I grew to love that one.

I grew to love my fears
of the dark lives that moved
in there; the black-haired witch
with huge breasts swinging deep
inside a thinning vest
over man's belt and trousers.

I only saw her when she swept
the quilt of dead leaves off her step
while a great ogre at the window,
in motley stains and buttons,
fag in mouth, shouted 'Come in
you hag,' shouted and wept.

Once a slow motion gin bottle
exploded under me and plucked
the spokes as I biked past,
'Get off my pavement, bastard!'
No blood or punctures proved
me invulnerable.

Still, I was nervous when he loomed
in suit and hat and buttonhole
outside the barber's where I'd propped
my guy. He dropped me sixpence
'for Guy fucking Fawkes'. I knew
then that my love was doomed.

On his way home from a long sup
he smiled. I liked my street now
without fear or risk of love.
He slipped me half-a-crown,
'And may you blow the whole
of bloody Parkstone up.'

This Is Our House

Door's smaller than the windows and shut tight,
roof swells like sea, chimney's a tall cigar,
path twists like smoke between the starry flowers.
Beside the house a woman stands up straight,
her yellow hair would fill the whole top floor.
This is our house, I done it just for you.

People won't fit inside, the child knows that.
Ground floor is clenched around a chuckling fire,
bedrooms billow with dreams, attic is fat
with dark that won't leak from the chimney-pot,
the child knows that. She'll try, her with the hair,
to get back in and clean it through and through.

KICKING SAWDUST

'When circus comes to town, the town dreams itself.'

to the memory of Philip Astley who in 1768
stood on horseback and traced the first modern ring

Ring-Master

Outside my canvas let the tempest roar!
At the still centre of this ring I prosper,
doff my top-hat, conjure my creatures' best.
Anarchy's ordered here. I'm self-possessed.
But on stark nights or stormy matinees
tent creaks, poles groan and guys grow mutinous;
fearful I'll lose my touch, loosen my grip,
I bind thongs to my wand and make a whip.

Fat Bearded Lady

I make a deep impression on the mud
of circus sites and on the gaping crowd
that shuffles through the turnstile to my booth
paying for generosity, for girth
and for the gall to show what they'd conceal
like secret sin beneath a cloak or shawl.
They hardly displace air. I laugh to see
them smirk and preen their slight normality.

Trapeze Artists

We swing like careless children, but sky-high:
work ourselves up, let ourselves go, and fly
or feint and seem to fall to make them gasp
and greedily gaze upwards as we grasp
pendulums that precisely intermesh
while, in the pit, drums roll and cymbals crash
swelling, as one, the public's appetite
like a fat spider in the safety net.

Lion-Tamer

To spare the rod would be to spoil the lion.
I spoil him with red meat and comb his mane;
sometimes he smiles, or curls his snarling lip
and prowls about our cage with hackles up.
His rank breath gives me the sharp taste of truth
each time I stuff my face into his mouth.
I trust my luck, my lion, keep my head
and a tame marksman who can shoot him dead.

Knife-Thrower

I have two aims. She has fine flesh, and trust
but blinks when I wink, Double-top? I lust.
Blindfolds, spread-eagle-spins, blades and close shaves.
We hold hands when we bow, then as she gives
me one coy kiss to please the audience
I smell her sweat, and wish she had more scents.
I love her faith, but long for her to feel
at closer range, warmer than naked steel.

Fire-Eater

You laugh at fear, but duck when sawdust's thrown;
buckets of water douse the grinning clown.
We fly through air, or poise above an earth
that's hand in glove with gravity and death.
You gasp. We're in our element. Mine's fire.
I spew it, suck it, scald my mouth, singe hair;
no miracles, no Phoenix, just a spark
of old Prometheus or young Joan of Arc.

Juggler

The thought of keeping things up in the air
is simple and not easy. With a flair
for physics and pure physicality
I lend the practice blithe facility.
Elementary particles in orbit –
balls, flaming torches, furniture, clubs, fruit
have gravity; but my charmed hands exult,
just let things slip to make it difficult.

Strong Man

I am Sisyphus in leopard's clothing
with an uphill task: to conquer loathing,
grip the audience, snatch and jerk the weights.
My corset ruptures underneath my spots,
iron bars are scarfs, directories are torn
in twos, weaklings with kids applaud. Deep down,
they say, a hard-man is a gentle soul.
I'd lift and bend and rend them once for all.

Acrobats

A springboard and unparalleled physique
build little empires; with refined technique,
tough discipline, top-men and underdogs,
we leap and grip like frenzied mating frogs.
Despite the sweat, each human hieroglyph
looks cool, almost abstract: successive
triangles chalked up and wiped like Euclid's,
noble and useless as the pyramids.

Snake-woman

My constrictor's like a feather boa
that tickles me a little, nothing more.
The crowd's hugely amused, it's not quite nice
to see them so aroused. Snakes, chill as ice
but drier than men's skin, can stir or scare
them stiff. They leer and take me for a whore.
My serpents flatter me with their clear gaze;
I'm almost happy in a cool embrace.

Pickpocket

My victim volunteers and will submit
to the relief of braces, watch and wallet.
They applaud him, the scapegoat to be fleeced,
and me as each fresh crime is witnessed,
egging me on to take the liberty
of making public private property.
But as they exit they hold raincoats close,
outside the tent fear every kind of farce.

Midget

My stature makes me stand out in a crowd,
father and peer to every little kid.
In the Big Top I make my way, happy
like any showman when they clap me;
I whirl, a dwarfish dervish, on the mat
as well as any long-limbed acrobat
but wish I tumbled further when I fall,
wish I could stride unstilted, could walk tall.

Band Leader

I've my baton, the ring-master his whip,
he rules the space but time is mine to keep:
I underscore each auguste clown's pratfall,
each tumbler's leap. Some will risk heart and soul
for the crowd's roar; my lads grudge lip and lung,
they'd play their socks off and remain unsung.
Crescendo. Kids' eyes are full of wonders,
fuller because my music fills their ears.

Human Cannonball

Though worn thin, keen to miss death by inches,
what artiste of my calibre flinches
at sliding down into the cannon's throat?
Held in its deafening hush I meditate.
I am attuned to the band's pulse, distant
but reassuring, till my assistant
springs me. Punched out into the world, I pause
safe in the net's embrace, and milk applause.

Clown

I am an artist playing to the mass,
the melancholy master on his arse.
To buckets, planks, each simple particle
I am the grand uncertain principal.
I grow refined, my props stay on the shelf,
against the world I pit merely myself
though one night, overweened with booze and pride,
I left the greasepaint off and children cried.

Sword-Swallower

I am a dietician. Sharp flavours
tempt my trained palate and oesophagus.
It sickens folk to see that I don't retch
but gobble short swords, long swords with despatch,
taking each down to drum-rolls through clenched teeth.
People delight in my distaste for death,
my appetite. On their behalf I crave
the lethal blade and swallow it, and live.

Bareback Rider

I ride of course, but really I'm the box.
I take the tickets, and the bloody knocks
if bunce and stubs don't tally. Musn't whinge,
but I'm supposed to check it and then change
to risk my neck and whatnot, round and round.
Horses are nice. My feet don't touch the ground.
The strong-man's a wet fart. My man's a clown,
got our own trailer now. It's not much fun.

Tight-rope Walker

Old acrobat, I balance, belly full
of long-drawn battles with the sawdust's pull,
the flex and tug of arms jutting at air
like a drunk clutching at the furniture;
I win applause, not equilibrium,
exhausting pose and then the long climb down.
I want an act I know I can keep up,
the poise of a hanged man on his tight rope.

Stilt-Walker

I condescend to give away balloons
then dwindle like a spire. Lofty buffoons
and elephants must lead the grand parade
to show off the dimensions of our trade:
your usual one-two-three, and less, and more,
down-at-heel freaks, athletes, fools on the floor.
Proud and precarious, we build big nights
while stray balloons cluster above the lights.

Elephant-girl

My spangled tail-coat's torn, my hat is flat,
my hair flies loose, the heel's come off one boot,
plinths crumble like anthills beneath the load
of antic elephants, who charge the crowd
plucking up poles like palms so sky falls down
as they dance quick-step, trumpeting in tune,
grey rocks or clouds that crush me like a worm.
Before we hit the road I get this dream.

Ringmaster

I have bowed out, music and lights have died,
we strike the ring and watch our world subside
with one languorous sigh. The king-pole's felled.
There is no wake, just work. I too, toppled
from king to jack, king-pin to handy-man,
hustler and clerk who pays the rent and then
moves on to hire things, turns and pastures new,
leaving a ring of bleached grass to the dew.

Captive

Now I know well it was a fantasy
that made me think art could be made into
an idol or a king.

MICHELANGELO SONNET LXV
(trans. Elizabeth Jennings)

The finishing, my midwife's touch:
the marble hulk Simone botched
delivered by my vision. This thing
the David, an idol or a king.

But Soderini, clerk of works,
thinks David's nose too coarse.
I grab a fistful of waste grit;
my conceit, to chime the mallet
and trickle chippings down.
The chisel's edge caresses stone
and does not mark it. *Enough,*
enough! That's made him live.

*   *   *

I put down patrons beneath marble tombs;
squabbles with them and all their praise
like wasters on my workshop floor.
I work upwards, until it seems
tears course the stone or seep through tempera.

Art's not an idol; or a king
to judge the short and the long days.
No, not the first dying,
the second death makes me crave grace.

*   *   *

I flay the dead, disinter men
from rock and strive to take them captive.

Think of the whitest winter of my youth,
courtyard of the Medicis, Piero
with an urgent, insolent commission:
chapped hands packed soft stuff,
life and art are brief.
I built an idol or a king of snow.

46

Release from Rome

(after Vasari)

One iron bedstead with its straw paliasse, one counterpane
of lambswool, blankets, a long grey dressing-gown and a locked chest
in the room in which he used to sleep.

It is now three in the morning and he is fully conscious
with good understanding but very sleepy, a drowsiness
he constantly tries to shake off, and tonight he yearned to ride
as every evening of fine weather.

A working forge squats in the loggia beside two bellows,
thick-set logs, a cask for oats or corn; in the stable a small
chestnut horse with saddle and bridle.

It is a Monday in carnival time. From the great black hearth
a blaze flickers in the creases of his face and swaddling clothes;
he sweats and shakes and will not go up to work through the dark hours,
a tallow candle strapped to his head.

One sketched-in statue of St Peter, one rough pietà
in broken marble, and a small unfinished Christ bearing his cross
in the low chamber under the roof.

Unbridled, the chestnut horse stamps and shuns its provender.
It is Friday. The master feebly, firmly says: I leave my soul
in God's hands, flesh to earth, goods to family; friends, remind me
now of the sufferings of Jesus.

Now, the unlocked chest gives up almost eight thousand scudi
and numerous sketches of plans for St Peter's. The body is laid
in the church of the Holy Apostles

but, lovingly cradled in a bale of wool, is smuggled out to Florence
from under the Pope's nose. While friends weep over sonnets
written in tears in his own hand, horse strains, cart groans,
bones shake I think with laughter.

Poet in Paradise

(St Giles Cripplegate 1790)

> *Ill fare the hands that heaved the stones*
> *Where Milton's ashes lay,*
> *That trembled not to grasp his bones*
> *And steal his dust away!*
>
> WILLIAM COWPER

Like digging up the devil
it was when we uncovered
his dessicated coffin

We bent to our mortal toil
for the church must be repaired
and the overseers want coin

A corpse for the Commonweal
this John's ripe to be plundered
who survived Restoration

Rough barber-surgeons we pull
teeth and pluck hair from a head
silted with darkened vision

Unholy relics for sale
to any rascal or lord
the rest's our exhibition

We show dust and bones and skull
picture of the disinterred
entitled Poet in Heaven

We've hollow bellies to fill
and he's neither breath nor bread
to lose and nothing to regain

Unfinished

*(Self-portrait by George Romney painted for
the poet William Hayley at Eartham in 1782)*

He asks you for your likeness, so you sit
putting yourself on canvas stroke by stroke,
your shifty mirror-image staring back
firmly, if faintly shocked by its self-doubt.

He begs you not to take the portrait home,
he owns its faulty and unfinished truth;
your qualms – a sketchy chair, a smudged backcloth
and falsely-folded arms – won't shake his claim.

Unmanned by praise, you leave yourself and go
back to your London studio's aura
of objective flattery, the sublime
caught and paid for. You and the poet know
that varnish is not vanity, nor are
sonnets perfected by the final rhyme.

Somme Simmons

Mr Simmons this forenoon paid us a visit, in so complete a metamorphosis...
CAPTAIN J.K. TUCKEY
Narrative of an Expedition to Explore the River Zaire, 1816

Mr Simmons is a good man, a sailor
I received at Deptford from the flagship,
paid off on the reduction of the fleet.

At Lombee, his father and his brother
came aboard our sloop and greeted him
with transports of joy, excessive ardour.

Christian Smith remarked these as evidence
that even amongst this people
nature is awake to tender emotions.

I noted that Simmons' ideas did not
assimilate to theirs; he persisted
in wearing his trousers and jacket.

He was reserved, though all night long
Lombee resounded with the din
of drums and songs of rejoicing.

His father, Mongova Seki, had entrusted
him, aged nine, to a Liverpool captain
for passage to England and education.

'To learn to make book,' he said; but
his guardian found it less troublesome
to sell him to make sugar on St Kitts.

Simmons escaped to a British Navy ship
and served the King in our late wars;
his father waited for him eleven years.

Now he serves the King of Boma, and us,
as fluent interpreter and diplomat
taking our oath on delicate matters.

This forenoon he comes in a silk coat
sewn with silver, over dirty shift and trousers;
a black glazed hat with grenadier feather

and the silk sash I gave him, supporting
a ship's cutlass; borne in a hammock
by two slaves, an umbrella shading him.

During our passage he performed
with no sign of impatience or disgust
the menial office of cook's mate.

Single Track

(Elizabethville 1915)

*What is the good of telling this man you can send your thoughts
thousands of miles by telegraph when he thinks you may have no real
thoughts to send? Or where is the utility of travelling by train fifty miles
an hour when you may have no real reason for taking the journey?*
DAN CRAWFORD
Back to the Long Grass

Handful of railcars
travelling south
coffins and doctors
ready for death

Nothing will happen
for five hours yet
future collision
present regret

Word tapped down the line
and word flew back
two trains are steaming
on the single track

No one can stop them
blinding through bush
a clerk stares at blame
at the far-off crash

Nothing can happen
for three hours yet
future collision
present regret

The third train's speeding
with time to spare
equipped for a meeting
and parting down there

Time for too many plans
premature griefs
three o'clock coffins
for eight o'clock stiffs

Nothing will happen
for an hour yet
future collision
present regret

All that can be done
going as planned
only this third train
knows journey's end

Handful of waggons
rolling on south
doctors and coffins
waiting for death

Lament

(Lusengo, Zaïre)

Ah, mama Ewoyo, you are cold.
There will be buyers for your dried fish
For your smoked monkey, but no seller:
Ah, mama Ewoyo, you are cold.

By my bed a mantis prayed all night
And my sweat flowed like the great river;
By yours, traders spread their hands and wailed:
Ah, mama Ewoyo, you are cold.

At dawn canoes came, fought our bow-wave
To make fast, with *kwanga*, crocodile,
But your stock needs no replenishing:
Ah, mama Ewoyo, you are cold.

Beside a forest village we moored,
Gave money towards your funeral;
A man swung an adze, others dug deep:
Ah, mama Ewoyo, you are cold.

A woman with heavy breasts, grass skirt
Walked round the hole, a soldier watched
Your raw box borne by many hands:
Ah, mama Ewoyo, you are cold.

At the top of the Congo's great bend
Half a day, then rattles, chants and prayers
And a spade passed strong arm to strong arm:
Ah, mama Ewoyo, you are cold.

Ah, mama Ewoyo, you are cold.
There will be buyers for your dried fish
For your smoked monkey, but no seller:
Ah, mama Ewoyo, you are cold.

Luminous Lover

(Ottawa 1922)

Luminous lover
I kissed her fine
and I've kissed her now
for the very last time

Oh I loved the lips
of my painter girl
as she sucked her brush
to a pointed curl

I'd stack and sweat
deep in the store
jealous of her painting
on the factory floor

Clocks and watches
coming down the line
always said she painted
to pass the time

Painted all the numbers
from twelve to one
big hands and little hands
luminous green

And I loved the lips
of my painter girl
as she sucked her brush
to a pointed curl

Through the Depression
we earned good pay
had a real high time
my lover and I

On early turn late turn
turning all the while
more than a hand's turn
at Radium Dials

Now I turn in my bed
in the lonely night
staring out the time
the time's so bright

Dream how the girls
made up for a laugh
with luminous eyebrows
lipstick and teeth

And I loved the lips
of my painter girl
as she sucked her brush
to a pointed curl

So open wide
say Ah! if you can
swell up your cheeks
put out your tongue

Too many sick ones
too many dead
quinsy or diptheria
the doctors said

They paid off the doctors
paid attorneys too
we couldn't prove nothing
nothing we could do

Now the factory's gone
bright times have passed
it's a parking lot
where the geiger ticks fast

Oh I loved the lips
of my painter girl
as she sucked her brush
to a pointed curl

My luminous lover
I kissed her fine
and I've kissed her now
for the very last time

Ouija Bawd

Get a straight answer? Not so lucky.
Is she in heaven (I didn't say hell)?
The shout should be simple *yes, ja, oui*
for she's never at home when I ring her bell
but the glass on the ouija board scuttles to *G*
and scrapes towards *R*, beginning to growl,
then stutters in limbo *A...V...E*
though that one was never Maria, but Nell.

Big Nell for the nonce, who can't say *nein*;
her *oui* hardens men and brings her low –
she loves a bad ponce and likes a bad pun
and plays with the play in words like *blow*,
like *bondage* or *stiff*, like *I'll give you one*.
All I get's no reply, or else the no-go:
She's tied up now, yes, yes, she's lying down.
The tumbler's still. This ouija is a no-no.

When Waves Give Up Their Dead

(*Royal Adelaide, Chesil Bank, 25 November 1872*)

When the sea gives up her dead it will be a host uncountable who will crowd the steep sides of the amphitheatre of Deadman's Bay.
FREDERICK TREVES

And when the waves give up their dead
I'll dance on the grinding shore
to watch the Royal Adelaide
and hear the pebbles roar

She tried to beat out of the bay
all that afternoon befogged
and fighting a sou'westerly
until her anchors dragged

So here's a landfall everyone
here's a gale to warp the stars
all on the London-Sydney run
poor emigrants and tars

Soon after dark it was she struck
broadside on the pebble ridge
2,000-ton clipper-built barque
hard by the Ferry Bridge

Tar barrels, torches, flares were lit
ghostly hills of water fell
upon a ship that soon must split
it was a glimpse of hell

Sailors with lanterns ran on deck
swung like dolls against a hull
that shuddered, lurched and snuffed their spark
flesh and stones, bone and skull

A force that nothing could outrun
took the ship up in its fists
cracked ribs, snapped spars and one by one
snipped off her masts

We gathered on the Chesil Bank
saw her rigging churned like wrack
and sensed her anguish as she sank
and felt her break her back

Victims screamed but no one heard
as spume burst in the vessel's shell
and shook the stones on which we stood
it was a snatch of hell

When flotsam spirits bumped ashore
kegs were broached to toast her crew
each spilt long rations down his maw
and down each others' too

So here's a windfall, here's a wake
here's a gale to steal your breath
and with a life-long thirst to slake
we drank ourselves to death

At dawn the storm-clouds went aground
gulls croaked and curious dogs
nuzzled the sexless ageless drowned
and revellers cold as logs

Their ship came home and so did mine
all foundered in that gale
when some of us sank too much brine
some too much alcohol

I'll swill rum yet at Ferry Bridge
by the ghostly Adelaide
and dance along the rattling ridge
when waves give up their dead

Struck

Not liking women much, I knew I'd stick
at home, upright and strong to run the farm
thinking that as you aged, dad, you'd retire
from field and yard back to the kitchen range
where mother and the kettle sang all day.
Her dead, I thought you'd tidy, wash and cook
while I made money selling milk and beef.
That's how it was before the lightning struck.

I stick at home. Outside I lean and look
at the horizon just one field away;
what land we haven't sold you hedge and ditch,
I stack the sticks or creosote the shed.
Inside all's shine, soap, disinfectant.
We make do on the Pension and the Sick
plus wily deals you do on market day,
stay proud despite the fact that lightning struck.

Twisted and crochety, I curse the muck
your boots bring in; shriek that your dinner's cold;
all weathers, air my washing at the stove;
send you, all weathers, out to smoke your pipe.
I'm mother here, since one bolt felled the cow
I milked, corkscrewed my spine and seared my back.
You scrub hands twice a day and dress the wound
that's not stopped weeping since the lightning struck.

Lane's End

The farm gate rattles,
mostly it's the wind.
One track into the world
the distance like a wall
the space a prison, acres
whose harvests come and come
and come to mock me here.
Him, his skin like earth
trespassing in my bathroom.
His granaries, for all he sucks
from bottles, richly swelling
and his man, young man
who has a life
because he lives elsewhere.
Their arms rest on my table
their silences agree
and exile me again.

I could break something
silence, teapot, vows.
I talk day long
calling myself to order
order against the tide
of straw and mud and shit
and my dark blood.
I twitch the sheets tight
on our mattresses.
I twit him and I tempt
kind words from his young man.
Something must disagree.
Across the fields the chapel
the hay-bed in the barn
the bottle by my pillow
that does not swill like his
but rattles, rattles.

Hugh Bullen Smithy

(for John Clemens's 85th birthday)

1

Light, like lichen clinging to a sapling's
leeward side, climbs on an upright pole
and human shadows thrown high up the wall
suggest a strong late sun set up in, say,
1907 by the photographer
together with his tripod, box, bulb, cowl.

An unseen door leads to the yard where horses
jostle the sunlight on their flanks and stamp
spent shoes. Welsh coals burn hotly without flame:
core of a forge sluiced now with bellows' drone,
now with water from a pail. Steam, bright shards
struck from anvils, eyes' whites, iron new moons.

But here there's small pretence at trade, they pose.
The beast's eyes in the photograph are shut,
far right, a shadowy dog or cat.
Eight human eyes stare frankly at the lens
ambushed but unsurprised. Beneath its cloak
the shutter yawns and snaps and captures them.

2

John, in the room where you were born I write
and look out on the bungalow you've built.
The smithy is my garage and workshop:
it was a motor-works and then a store,
no trace of hearth or stack, just whitewashed stone
and concrete skim over its cobbled floor.

Poor lineage for the furnace that once fed
a great estate, until the gentry's line
died out, left railings, gates and carriage-wheels
to rot. Your memories, passed freely on,
have given me the sense of where I live,
of how it fenced and moved this part of Devon.

One memory, darkly framed, ten years beyond
this photograph: the night your father came home
hot from auction, outbid for both his hearths,
fears realised by three hammer blows upon
his heart's anvil. You, disinherited.
Each season, still, this ground gives up its iron.

3

As if they unbent briefly from the work
your father and his two apprentices
stand foursquare, arms slack but grasping hammers,
tongs, a finished shoe. The lads wear soiled shirts,
studs at the throat, braces and branded aprons,
cocky flat caps and mundane work-worn boots.

The smith's habit: waistcoat and bowler hat,
but Sunday boots religiously buffed up
make an occasion of the everyday
and the boy squatting on a sack of chaff
is decked out for the portrait studio
in breeches, Eton collar, handkerchief.

Scythe, rake and harness hang in the late sun:
backdrop of ordinary disorder
from which with serious eyes they turn and pose
to honour, not to falsify their lives.
Nothing is more mundane than passing years.
I celebrate your birthday, John, with this.

Living Down Here

(for John Clemens)

90°. In tall beech shade
the old farmer sits with his hat on
and celebrates the weather and the trees

with one reservation: how much higher
will they grow to overshadow
the bungalow he built for his old age?

Before that all this was field.
Here foresters dumped tree-tops,
a stock of logs and lightings,

a slow using-up of the wood
that stood here before it was field.
He burnt it, but left the seedlings

which planted themselves from that stack
of 1940. Here's neither wood nor field
but a garden where he sweats in deep shade.

He looks up through shoals of finny green,
plumbs fifty years of blue
and says this exactly:

Little did I think
when I saw those twigs
that I'd be living down here.

Ryme Intrinseca

(Dorset)

Modest village within the *rim*, or ridge,
which boasts that once it was the residence
of kings. Not much left now, beside the church,
doubly-restored medieval, to applaud:
an avenue of carefully clipped yew
shading the path, a rector's epitaph –
'Reader weep on his herse in whom did dwell
all vertues yet twas love made him excell.'
So I will mourn good bones, and the unborn
of Ryme Extrinseca, this place's twin
whose stones are lost, like rime in sun, like frost.

Even Keel

(Mousehole)

Here yelping gulls and gulping waves tousle
our dreams: we rouse, the split quay walls reveal
seamless sea-sky, St Michael's Mount unreal
in haze. Profound shoals sleep, await arousal.

St Clement's Isle repudiates with zeal
day's vanities and last night's carousal.
Granite is picturesque upon an easel
and Dolly's curses still please the genteel.

Bloody-minded beauty bids espousal
of both the base and the ethereal:
where black lace nets once shrouded the sea-wall
the igneous cliffs are lit by flame-blue squill
and wind leans at our ballast, out of Mousehole,
to speed us home upon an even keel.

Dolly Pentreath: one of the last true Cornish speakers, was famous for her
colourful language. She died at Mousehole (pronounced '*mousle*') in 1777
and her memorial at Paul was erected by Prince Lucien Bonaparte.

The Island

*She thinks of nothing but the Isle of Wight, and she calls it
the Island, as if there were no other island in the world.*
                    JANE AUSTEN,
                    Mansfield Park

Landfalls

The Solent River plundered by the ebb
long since; a relic of its southern shore
still tethered to the mainland by a web
of wake, above an oozy, scoured sea-floor
wreck-thick between the Needles and the Nab.
The hovercraft and hydrofoils' roar
drowns muffled rowlocks at Wight's back: each tub
importing treason's taint and draught of war.

The Island bobs like cork in history's tide.
Accomplices and enemies in France,
Spaniards, Jutes, Germans planned to override
the swell of chalk; English Victorians,
possessed by dreams of little empire, tried.
Still Wight, stiff-necked and broken-backed, will dance.

Enclaves

White stacks, a ring of forts turned fun-palace,
crease of Cretaceous Chalk pin-striped with flint,
a turf of miniatures – long undermined
by caverns, tunnels, shafts – crowned with a Cross
since Tennyson made for his beacon there.
His home in the soft heart, the pastel sands
which High Down's green unbreaking wave defends
against the shock of water, clout of air.

Paths lead from chalet-sprawl, up field, down copse
to Yar bank and a boatyard's busy hush,
scallop-tiled shop, fish glistering on slabs,
cauldrons to make the armoured lobster blush.
Around the Spit, the Solent sucks at clays,
flesh of West Wight prised from her carapace.

Reaches

No, stranger, it is not quite Alcatraz;
nor one great yacht marina, begging Cowes'
and millionaires-in-gin-palaces'
pardon. Newtown's no place for such bezazz.
Merchants' ghosts stir in Gold Street's swathe of grass,
the Town Hall's lost its town, so careless, yes,
though what's left boasts its Randy. Fairs like farce
vainly preserve old improprieties.

But shall we walk the Wall, see how the Creek
has lost and almost regained Paradise?
We'll plumb Clamerkin's reaches and Rodge Brook
to depths of Parkhurst where no curlew cries.
I'll lead you back through Cowes on seasoned roads
through trees, to bole and keel, to axe and adze.

Civilities

Creeks dammed for mills, streams channelled into leats;
Chillingwood, Deadman's, Blackbridge brooks seep down
from shreds of forest, their rearguard retreats;
wilderness civilised again, again.
Old stone-pits rest under a pall of green
near ruined Quarr, and black monks' praise now beats
against brick spans. The shade of a black Queen
taps out psychic tattoos, entreats, entreats.

Ryde's sprouting spires outsoar her vanity,
her pier leap-frogs mud, while Brading Haven's
spreading lap succumbs to land's advance;
the Fleet's repulsed, rings rust at a lost quay,
the Mayor's Dog baits no bulls. Flats squat, yachts prance
for us – our barbarous urbanity.

Axis

The long view, from Castle keep to Castlehold:
twin torrents once sliced through the Island's spine
and carved Carisbrooke's motte; waters that boiled
now trickle north to annex Newport town
and greet the tides which ride in from the world
to the Wight's heart, trade and war in their train.
All fluctuates, all treasons are repelled
but time's advance, down payment on each stone.

Power's tributaries run to lawlessness
through burghers', clerics', merchants', pirates' ground,
leaving Divine Right stranded behind bars.
Restored, decayed, rebuilt: the treadmill's round
where nothing keeps or holds, though time allows
the Castle like a trinket on its mound.

Riches

I clamber down the canyon of Whale Chine
to the red apron of the Bay of Death.
The tide worries at hulks of fossil pine,
withdraws with bones of reptiles in its teeth
and shifts old ballast towards Rocken End.
My head silts with sad tales, and tales untold
of legendary cargoes, foundering land
that tumbles at my back, panned, drowned Wight gold.

Inland, riches outcrop between the downs:
luminous fields like emeralds and ores,
clusters of boom-time Jacobean stones;
broad road to shores crusted with villas, bars
and neon piers on pins, whose antique pride
still takes the treacherous waters in its stride.

Tropics

On the saint's down a golden oriole flies
and Boniface's spring flits down, far south
to land-slipped latitudes luxuriant
enough to summon sonnets up; love-songs
whose rhythms, rhymes and stresses must embrace
rock's crack of doom, clay gouts on Undercliff,
diverted roads and streams, the deviant
genius loci of chalybeate springs.

Liquor floods in on the astringent tide,
stocks the long shelf where the infirm adore
their latest god. I breathe an elegy
to Ventnor, last resort on Styx's shore;
where genius thrived, graveyard geology
insists that all things ordinary died.

Anosmia
(for T.H.)

No nose for anything now.
He mourns the singular smell of fear
the plural scents of love. Subtle
losses grieve him, not bland flowers.

He eats, but misses the flavours,
piles sugar in his cup, salt
on his plate. He has a tongue for
memories, sourness and sweetness.

He tastes sweet rain upon cut grass
and the sea, he loves the sea,
the tides in the wind. Unsubtle
like sexual juice, like hot tears.

Seeing Her Across

Each weekday morning in term-time
    I walk to the main road,
my stick under my arm and warmth
    of my child's hand in mine.

She step-steps for each stride I make,
    she stops me at the curb;
we hear the cars, she looks both ways,
    squeezes my hand and runs.

Those who can see will understand
    each day holds its small loss.
I turn, my stick tap-taps back home
    from seeing her across.

Cumuli

The dream's just like real death.
Rain aslant between the digging
and the burial, the earth mound
glints with stones washed white,
they are not bones, and the grave's
clay floor glitters with rainwater
not tears. The coffin's solid wood.

Webs sigh, warming the bearers' hands.
Daffodils gleam upon cut stems
trumpeting a still-pristine tune.
The lid's a door, there is no bottom,
we could dive in and soar
through cumuli and the deep blue
where everything costs nothing.

Soberly dressed and briefly
we queue with our small change.
The door is fast. Earth flumps down
thickly and we must come home.

Granny's Gloves

(Digitalis alba)

The blackest thing about the snow fox
is its spoor, a devious dream
stalking the dense waste of the cortex

There, at the parting of grandmother's hair
through her thin scalp, I thought I saw
her fine face purpled and heart snared

Then 'Digitalis!' attack after attack
restored her pallor and damped fibrillations
each time but one the foxglove brought her back

These seeds will quicken, and slow grief
with quilted green, octaves of fingers
all her Edwardian summers' gloves

Much later, I can see her head of hair
watching the white globe of the moon
on TV, and the footprints there

'That's the moon, granny, men in space'
and she, 'Where are they really?'
Her pityingly indulgent gaze

It is an old tune their hearts strum
upon a figment of our gravity
up where the hare sleeps in its form

But she sees some north-polar comic turn
or flour-mill robots, not that lunar light
in which no foxgloves wax or wane

And I am seeing sutures, snow-fox track
stroking the white hair that I love
sensing the wild one double back, and back

Where starry flowers flank lanes too deep
for gigs to pass unscathed, she saw
thorn hedge-banks snatching at black crêpe

I see the purples nodding in her wake
and in the autumn I will plant capsules
of green, white heat for summer's sake

New Moon

(for Maggie)

Tonight it was important
to revisit the valley
where the bearded heron
is undisputed president

so we unlatched that gate
took the honeyed track
below beeches just extruded
into electric dusk

saw the bald outcrop bare
between tussocky sheep
where the venerable bird
should have been standing

still as a missile
above the shifting stream
but where it was not
a pale fox stared at us

pricked amongst fiery bracken
and a green woodpecker
took itself trunk to trunk
in a world we shall not revisit

from whose clouds of indigo
the new moon hung
a sharp hook sheer into
the peach plum rosehip sky

and caught our breath

The New Water-Music

The sun tumbles the shadows of things headlong,
wrings infra-red from boles and jagged reed-beds.
Duck, unreflecting, stand on the lake's skin
or touch down skittering and more ungainly
than the fifth generation of computers.

Sky-striding heron damps its neck's sine-wave.
The ice aches for catastrophe. My pratfalls prompt
geese to akimbo silent-movie rushes
at take-off. I, too, uncertain and more gauche
than the fifth generation of computers

with my tragic sense. My carelessly-flung stones
strike vacant ice and synthesise a music
of pure whiplashes – *faz-zang, faz-zong, faz-zung* –
worth more than these poor ears, this air, that sun,
worthy of chaos and equilibrium.

BLOODAXE POETRY HANDBOOKS: 1

Getting into Poetry
by PAUL HYLAND

This book helps readers, writers and teachers to hack their way into the jungle of contemporary poetry. It informs, demystifies, illuminates and excites. It gives a realistic account of the poetry scene in Britain and Ireland, corrects common misconceptions and allows young or new writers to see themselves in context. Paul Hyland has written the book he wanted to read when he started getting into poetry.

● **Modernists to Martians:** Groups, movements, fashions and influences. Jargon and hype: what it all means in plain English, from the ludic to the ludicrous.

● **Key books:** Which are the most important collections and the most influential anthologies? Which are the poems of our time?

● **Poetry readings:** The circuit and the circus. The importance of the ear, the power of the spoken word *versus* the ego-trip turn-off.

● **Getting into print:** The editor's eye view. Submitting to magazines and publishers. How to target editors and save time, paper and money.

● **Competitions and prizes:** Winning words. Competition poems. Do prizes lead to publication? Awards and bursaries.

● **Organisations:** Poetry societies, Arts Councils, regional arts boards. Who your allies are. How they help and how you should approach them.

● **Critical help:** Where you can get feedback and advice. Postal services, pundits and gurus. Courses, workshops and writers-in-residence.

● **Nice Little Earners:** Jobs poets can do. Readings, schools, residencies.

● **Resources:** A wealth of information and listings, together with provocative chapters on both Riches and Paranoia.

'Essential reading...*the* guide to the contemporary poetry scene' – TIME OUT

'Excellent...entertaining and demystifying advice to any would-be poet' – TIMES

'Anyone who seriously wants to be in the next new poets number ought to be reading this book now' – POETRY REVIEW

'Just about as comprehensive as you can get on the subject of breaking into the poetry world' – POETRY LONDON NEWSLETTER

'The fact that this deceptively slim volume has had rave reviews in a large number of poetry magazines is witness to the extent the author's intentions have been realised: namely to demystify the "poetry scene" in plain English' – NATE NEWS

'A survival guide to anyone actively interested in contemporary poetry' – WRITERS' NEWS